# ATTRACTING AND FEEDING HUMMINGBIRDS

Sheri Williamson

## Photo Credits:

**Ron Austing**: p. 10; 24 both; 26T & C; 45; 56T
**Guido Dingerkus**: p. 44
**Paul Freed**: p. 21 (Lyssomanes viridis)
**R. Brower Hall**: p. 58B
**Marvin Hyett**: p. 6; 16; 43; 59T
**Larry Kimball**: p. 1 (Rufous Hummingbird); 3 (Rufous Hummingbird); 11 (Rufous Hummingbird); 12T (Rufous Hummingbird); 14; 33; 54; 55 (Broad-tailed Hummingbird); 58T
**Larry Kimball & Barbara Magnuson**: p. 32 (Gambel's Oak)
**Peter LaTourrette**: p. 17; 47 (Anna's Hummingbird); 50; 57T & B
**Eric Loza**: p. 19T
**Barbara Magnuson**: p. 12B; 13; 26B; 27T; 51 (Broad-tailed Hummingbird); 57C
**Rafi Reyes**: p. 23; 27B; 36; 38
**Rob & Ann Simpson**: p. 4; 7; 9B; 15; 19B; 20; 25; 27C; 35 (Black-chinned Hummingbird); 39; 40; 46; 49; 52; 53; 56C & B; 59B
**T. Tilford**: p. 5 (Booted Racket-tail); 8
**John Tyson**: p. 34
**Sheri Williamson**: p. 9T; 18; 28; 29T & B; 30T & B; 31 all; 42; 48; 58C; 59C; 60 all; 61

## Dedication

To my husband and field companion, Tom Wood, and the birds that have enriched our lives beyond measure

KT 105

Distributed in the UNITED STATES to the Pet Trade by T.F.H. Publications, Inc., 1 TFH Plaza, Neptune City, NJ 07753; on the Internet at www.tfh.com; in CANADA by Rolf C. Hagen Inc., 3225 Sartelon St., Montreal, Quebec H4R 1E8; Pet Trade by H & L Pet Supplies Inc., 27 Kingston Crescent, Kitchener, Ontario N2B 2T6; in ENGLAND by T.F.H. Publications, PO Box 74, Havant PO9 5TT; in AUSTRALIA AND THE SOUTH PACIFIC by T.F.H. (Australia), Pty. Ltd., Box 149, Brookvale 2100 N.S.W., Australia; in NEW ZEALAND by Brooklands Aquarium Ltd., 5 McGiven Drive, New Plymouth, RD1 New Zealand; in SOUTH AFRICA by Rolf C. Hagen S.A. (PTY.) LTD., P.O. Box 201199, Durban North 4016, South Africa; in JAPAN by T.F.H. Publications. Published by T.F.H. Publications, Inc.

Manufactured in the

United States of America

by T.F.H. Publications, Inc.

# CONTENTS

LIVING JEWELS 5

1 HOW HUMMINGBIRDS LIVE 11

2 PUTTING OUT THE WELCOME MAT 21

3 FEEDING HUMMINGBIRDS 35

4 PROVIDING A SAFE HAVEN 47

5 SHARING THE GIFT OF HUMMINGBIRDS 51

6 A GUIDE TO HUMMINGBIRDS 55

RESOURCES 62

INDEX 64

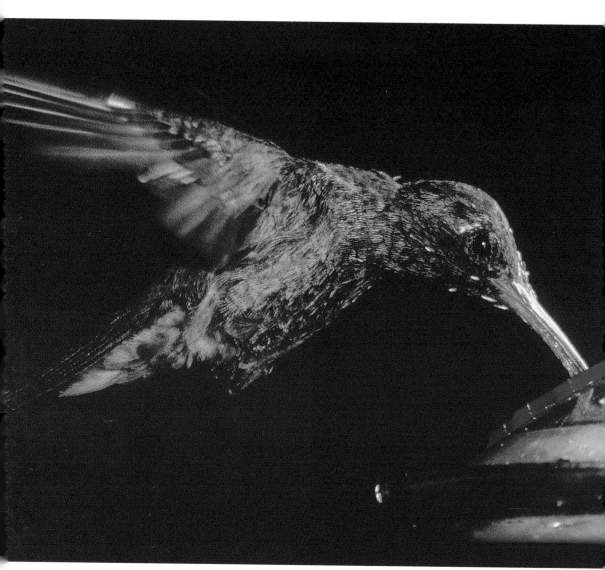

*A male Broad-billed Hummingbird at a feeder. This very dark southwestern species has an orange bill.*

*Introduction*

# LIVING
# JEWELS

America's two most popular outdoor activities are gardening and birding, and hummingbirds inspire equal devotion in both groups of enthusiasts. Exotic as they seem, these living jewels are as comfortable in suburban yards as in tropical forests. Their beauty and personality have earned them a place among the most beloved of all our native birds and the most welcome of all garden visitors. This guide will help you understand the fascinating and complex lives of hummingbirds and how to transform your yard or garden into a hummingbird haven.

Hummingbirds have captured the human imagination for thousands of years. With their tiny size,

*Costa's Hummingbird (immature) feeding. The high energy needs of hummingbirds control their lives, the birds following flower blooms all year.*

brilliant jewel-like colors, and fearless nature, they seem to bridge the gap between real animals and creatures of myth and legend. The first European explorers to write home about these improbable birds were often dismissed as liars or lunatics; after all, who had ever heard of a bird the size of an insect? The tiniest of all, the Bee Hummingbird, is actually outweighed by some insects and is the second smallest of all warm-blooded animals. The largest, the Giant Hummingbird of South America, is larger than many songbirds.

Even their flight is insect-like. Thanks to unique wing and shoulder anatomy, hummingbirds are the only birds able to hover in still air and fly backwards, sideways, straight up and down. In the normal flapping flight of most birds, the wings move mainly up and down, and only the downward stroke actually provides lift. In hovering flight, a hummingbird's wings move in a horizontal figure eight. This nearly doubles the lift and gives hummingbirds their maneuverability. Their wings also move at amazing speeds, from as low as 10 beats per second in the Giant Hummingbird to around 80 beats per second in some of the smallest species.

This type of flight requires an enormous amount of energy, most of which is supplied by the sugars in the flower nectar they drink. Even at rest, hummingbirds use so much energy that they would quickly overheat if not for their small body size, which rapidly dissipates excess heat. A human who burned calories at the rate of a hummingbird would literally cook from the inside from the heat generated. Like any athlete, a hummingbird needs plenty of oxygen, which is supplied by super-efficient lungs that circulate air in just one direction and is delivered to the muscles by the largest heart in proportion to body size of any bird.

With such high energy demands, hummingbirds could easily starve to death overnight were it not for the ability to dramatically reduce energy consumption when at rest. When under stress due to cold weather, lack of food, or the rigors of migration, a hummingbird can enter a hibernation-like state known as torpor. As night falls, its heart rate drops to as little as one-twentieth of normal, its body temperature falls to near

*The more than 300 species of hummingbirds known all are from the New World, Canada to southern South America plus the Caribbean islands. This is a female Purple-throated Mountain Gem photographed in Costa Rica.*

the temperature of the outside air, and its breathing may stop for minutes at a time. To a casual observer the bird might appear dead, but at first light it slowly emerges from this state and resumes normal activity.

One of the most captivating features of hummingbirds is their iridescent colors. These stunning metallic hues are produced not by pigment but by the way the feathers bend and reflect light. Microscopic structures in each feather act like a prism, breaking sunlight into its component colors then reflecting a single pure color back to the observer's eye. Unlike their pigment-based counterparts, iridescent colors can change dramatically depending on the angle of the light and the position of the observer. From different viewpoints, the throat of a male Rufous Hummingbird can appear black, scarlet, coppery, gold, or even chartreuse. In most North American species the male wears the brightest colors, refined over countless generations by the tastes of discriminating females.

Many Native American cultures hold hummingbirds in high regard as fearless and flamboyant warriors, a more perceptive view than our modern image of dainty flower-sipping sprites. Hummingbirds are also highly intelligent and curious. Their excellent memories allow them to relocate nest sites, flower patches, and feeders year after year. Many bird lovers tell of seeing the first hummingbird of the spring hovering in confusion at the spot where a feeder hung the previous summer. Occasional hummingbirds even seem to understand the connection

*Sunbirds, family Nectariniidae, are in some respects the Old World equivalents of American hummingbirds, having elongated bills for reaching into flowers and brilliant reflective colors. They are heavier birds that tend to feed while perched, however.*

between people and feeders, searching out and scolding the homeowner until the sugar water supply is replenished. Few other wild animals appear so comfortable living near humans, and fewer still are so well loved in return.

But although they have fans around the world, hummingbirds are found only in the Western Hemisphere. Approximately 320 species inhabit a wide variety of habitats, from the southern tip of South America to southeastern Alaska. Like many of our most colorful birds, hummingbirds are most at home in the tropics, and the closer you get to the equator, the more species you encounter. Ecuador, a South American country slightly larger than the state of Colorado, is home to more than 150 species of hummingbirds, more than ten times the number of species that nest in all of the United States and Canada.

*A female White-eared Hummingbird feeding from a wild tobacco plant in northern Mexico. Hummers are modified to feed within tubular flowers.*

Here in the United States, each region has a different mix of hummingbird species. Not surprisingly, the greatest variety exists along the Mexican border; as many as 15 species may visit the deserts and mountains of southeastern Arizona each season. Running a close second is the Gulf Coast region, with a list that includes wintering western hummingbirds and rare strays from the tropics. Along the Pacific Coast, many gardens host Anna's Hummingbirds all year and up to five other species from spring through fall. The mountainous regions of the West are home to two to four species, including nesting Broad-tailed and Calliope Hummingbirds. The eastern parts of the United States and Canada are home to a single nesting species, the Ruby-throated, but occasional strays of western species such as Rufous and Black-chinned keep bird lovers on the alert during migration.

*Female Green-crowned Brilliants photographed in Costa Rica. The dozen-plus species of hummingbirds that nest in the U.S. and Canada don't compare with the diversity in most tropical countries from Mexico south.*

*A female Ruby-throated Hummingbird with her two young.*

*Chapter One*

# HOW HUMMINGBIRDS LIVE

## Migration

The lives of most familiar hummingbirds are one long travelogue. To escape the intense competition in the tropics, they travel as far north as southern Canada and Alaska each spring to nest, then return south at the end of summer. The long-distance record holder is the Rufous Hummingbird, which winters in northern and central Mexico and nests as far north as southeastern Alaska. Individual Rufous that nest at the northern edge of the species' range must make a one-way trip of at least 2,700 miles twice each year, the equivalent of a human traveling around the world one and three-quarters times.

*Rufous Hummingbirds may migrate 2,700 miles each way every year of their lives. This female is feeding at penstemon flowers.*

Equally remarkable is the feat performed each spring by Ruby-throated Hummingbirds. Along with millions of migratory songbirds, these tiny creatures follow a direct but dangerous route across the Gulf of Mexico, from the Yucatan Peninsula of Mexico to the Gulf Coast of the United States, on their way to eastern nesting grounds. This journey over more than 500 miles of open water is fueled by stored fat, often up to two-thirds of the bird's normal body weight.

Migratory hummingbirds must time their travels to coincide with the bloom season of their flowers, departing before the first killing frosts of fall. Fortunately, the urge to migrate is triggered not by cold or hunger but by changing day length. The shorter days of midsummer trigger chemical changes in the birds' brains, creating a restlessness that soon leads to departure for the wintering grounds. These changes also trigger a feeding frenzy, which helps the birds build reserves of energy-rich fat as insurance against the uncertainties of migration. Males often head south while females are still tending young. The first southbound male Rufous Hummingbirds arrive in western Mexico at the beginning of the rainy season in early July, before some of the resident Mexican species have begun nesting.

The journey itself is guided by an internal compass, which in adults is aided by memories of landmarks along the route. Unlike geese, cranes, and other social birds, young hummingbirds make their first migration alone, with no help from their elders. Weather, insufficient food supplies, predators, and other hazards take a particularly heavy toll

*Male hummingbirds commonly migrate south while females are still brooding, and immatures must take their first trip south by themselves. Here a female Rufous feeds on thistle in Colorado.*

on the young, but those that survive their first migration may repeat it annually over the same routes for more than ten years.

## Hummingbirds and Their Flowers

One of the most intriguing aspects of hummingbirds is their relationship with the flowers they pollinate. Plants can't go in search of a mate, so to ensure cross-pollination many plant species bribe animals to act as matchmakers. Like bees, butterflies, moths, and other pollinators, hummingbirds pick up quantities of pollen each time they visit a flower, and this is carried to the next flower in turn. The plant pays for these services in the sugar-rich nectar that powers the birds' high-energy lifestyle. Hummingbirds are particularly good pollination partners for plants that live in cool, cloudy, or shady environments where cold-blooded insects are at a disadvantage.

Hummingbirds aren't the only birds that drink nectar, but they are the only ones that can hover at flowers. This adaptation helped them colonize the temperate zones of North America, where the abundant insect-pollinated flowers were too fragile to support the weight of even the smallest bird. Most of our North American hummingbird flowers descended relatively recently from insect-pollinated ancestors and still resemble them. In contrast, many tropical flowers that have had much longer relationships with hummingbirds are even more specialized in anatomy, color, and nectar content.

Penstemon cf. eatonii, *a snapdragon relative, serves as a nectar source for a female Broad-tailed Hummingbird. Hummingbirds prefer nectars with high sucrose content, not more simple sugars.*

13

Though they must compete with each other for pollinators, plants economize by limiting nectar production. This means that a hungry hummingbird can quickly empty even a large patch of flowers. With such high energy requirements, hummingbirds can't afford to share their limited resources, and this leads to their characteristic territorial squabbles. In most of the smaller species, the male establishes and defends a territory covering enough flowers to meet his energy needs. Territories are smaller where flowers are abundant, larger where they are scarce. Though hummingbirds are territorial year round, fighting is most intense during the early nesting season, when the quality of a male's territory may affect his mating opportunities. The battles diminish prior to the southward migration, when fattening up is the first priority and fighting would waste valuable feeding time.

*The pollen on the bill of this Black-chinned Hummingbird will be transferred to the next flower on which she feeds, helping ensure that food plants are pollinated.*

In some larger hummingbird species, the preferred strategy, called "traplining," is to go from one flower patch to another along a regular route, driving away the territory holder if necessary to gain access to the nectar. Very small species may take the stealthy approach, darting in quietly to feed while the dominant bird's back is turned. Research has shown that hummingbirds learn not only which plants supply the most nectar but how long it takes the plant to replenish its nectar supply. During this interval a territorial bird will continue to guard the plant but won't waste time trying to feed; "trapliners" will simply time their visits to coincide with the plants' "delivery" of a fresh supply of nectar.

But nectar is far from a complete diet, with little more nutritional value than a soft drink. For essential nutrients such as proteins, vitamins, and minerals, hummingbirds must feed on insects, spiders, and other invertebrates. These tiny predators capture gnats and flies on the wing, glean aphids and leafhoppers from the leaves and stems of plants, and pluck spiders from their own webs. Larger hummingbirds have proportionally lower energy requirements than smaller species and tend to be more insectivorous, often taking nectar only in the early morning, late evening, and during inclement weather. When flowers are scarce, as in early spring, hummingbirds may depend primarily on insects for weeks at a time. Some have even learned that the tree sap that oozes from holes made by sapsuckers is a sweet, nutritious supplement until the flowers come into bloom.

*A male Anna's Hummingbird. Male hummingbirds generally have brilliant reflective throat feathering (gorgets) that is poorly developed or absent in females, at least in U.S. species.*

## Courtship and Nesting

Once settled on their nesting grounds, hummingbirds quickly go about the business of reproduction. The female bears the entire burden of building the nest and caring for the young, with no help from the male. His primary responsibility is to impress females in search of fathers for their children, and he will mate with as many females as he can. In many other birds, the relationship between male and female may last a lifetime, but in hummingbirds it rarely lasts more than a few minutes.

The male is usually the first to arrive on the breeding grounds, where he promptly sets about selecting and defending a choice territory. From a conspicuous perch, he surveys his domain for both rivals and prospective mates. In many species, such as Anna's, the male will also sing to advertise his presence. These songs are usually little more than raspy twitters, hardly comparable to the musical delights performed by warblers, orioles, and other songbirds, but the basic message is the same.

In hummingbirds, the line between courtship and aggression is a blurry one. In species such as Ruby-throated, Black-chinned, Anna's, and Rufous, a territorial male will greet interlopers of either sex with a spectacular dive display, often accompanied by special calls or sounds made by air rushing over the wings and tail. If the intruder is female and doesn't immediately beat a hasty retreat, the male will close in for a more intimate display, the shuttle flight. Flying back and forth in short arcs in front of or just above the female, the male shows off his brilliant colors. If the female is unimpressed or simply not interested in mating, she may

*Female hummingbirds (here a Costa's) may be relatively dull and often are difficult to identify. Males may recognize females by their behavior when challenged as much as by their coloration.*

flee with the male in close pursuit or even turn and attack him. The mating act itself is rarely observed but may take place in a shrub or tree, on the ground, or even in flight.

By the time she goes in search of a mate, the female has already constructed her nest. Lined with soft plant fibers and animal hair to cushion and insulate the eggs and nestlings, the entire nest structure is held together and attached to its support using one of the strongest materials in existence: spider silk. The sticky strands that entrap the spider's prey bond to each other, the lining material, and the support. By layering silk and fiber, the female creates a strong, lightweight cup that fits snugly around her body during incubation but stretches with the rapidly growing young. The female may camouflage the

*Hummingbirds build tiny, expandable nests for their two eggs, holding the whole thing together with spider webs. This female Black-chinned seldom leaves her nest for the 13 to 16 days the eggs are incubating.*

outside of the cup with bits of lichen, moss, or plant debris to conceal it from predators; this is so effective that few people have ever seen a hummingbird nest in the wild. The typical nest site is in a tree or shrub sheltered from above by an overhanging branch or large leaf. However, some female hummingbirds have a flair for the exotic, building their nests in caves, under bridges, in potted plants, on wind chimes, or attached to hanging chains or ropes.

The female lays two (very rarely one or three) white eggs about one day apart. For the next 12 to 18 days she spends most of her time incubating, leaving the nest only to eat, drink, bathe, and gather additional material for the nest. In northern and mountainous regions where overnight temperatures often dip below freezing even in summer, hummingbirds may go into torpor to conserve energy on cold nights. A nesting female must maintain a high enough body temperature to prevent her eggs or young from becoming fatally chilled, so she must burn energy at near daytime rates even on frosty nights.

The hatchlings, each about the size of a honeybee, are blind and virtually naked, with wispy tufts of down on their heads and backs. Unlike most other young birds, they are silent until they leave the nest. They don't need to cry to let their mother know they're hungry—they're always hungry! The tiny nestlings instinctively open their mouths when they feel the wind from their mother's wings or the touch of her bill on their backs. The female takes aim at their yellow gapes and plunges her rapier-like bill into their crops, seeming to pin them to the nest. From her own crop she regurgitates a slurry of predigested insects and nectar, rich food for the growing chicks. During this vulnerable time, the female is always on guard against potential predators and will attack snakes, lizards, squirrels, jays, and even humans that threaten her nest.

As the chicks' feathers appear, the female spends less time at the nest and more time foraging to satisfy their growing appetites. By the time the nestlings are fully feathered, the nest is nearly worn out, and the young tightly grip its sagging rim as they try their new wings. Finally, after 18 to 28 days in the nest, one youngster will take its first flight, usually with the second close behind. At this stage of life the young hummingbirds are almost fully grown, but they will still be dependent on their mother for a week or more. For the first few days the fledglings sit inconspicuously in a shrub or tree, peeping to attract their mother's attention. As they gain strength and confidence, they will follow her to food sources, water, etc., learning what they'll need to survive on their own.

The end of summer signals the next great adventure in the life of a young hummingbird: its first southward migration. An innate calendar and compass tell it when to leave and what direction to

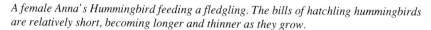

*A female Anna's Hummingbird feeding a fledgling. The bills of hatchling hummingbirds are relatively short, becoming longer and thinner as they grow.*

*Snakes such as this gopher snake are among the many predators of hummingbirds, and they sometimes are attracted to feeders.*

travel, but the rest of the journey is a learning experience. If it survives the hardships of migration and finds a safe winter refuge, chances are good that the following spring it will return to the area where it hatched, ready to take its place in the breeding population.

Though hummingbirds can live more than ten years, for most species studied so far the average life span in the wild is around five years. Weather probably plays the biggest role in hummingbird mortality. Birds of any age may succumb to starvation if drought or cold weather reduces the availability of nectar and insects, and summer hailstorms may kill both mothers and their young. Eggs and nestlings are particularly vulnerable to predators such as jays, squirrels, and snakes. Adults occasionally fall prey to small hawks or owls, large flycatchers, or praying mantises, or become entangled in spider webs. Newly independent youngsters must compete with aggressive, experienced adults for food while they learn how to forage and escape predators. Though hummingbirds don't normally fight to the death, injuries they receive in combat may increase their vulnerability to predators or prevent them from migrating.

*Squirrels not only attack hummingbird feeders, but they may break eggs and actually eat the nestlings in their nests.*

Added to these natural hazards are a gauntlet of man-made dangers, including habitat destruction, pesticides, domestic cats, windows, and transmission towers. Even exotic plants can be deadly. Burdock, a European weed with a flower head covered in hooked spines, has fatally ensnared untold numbers of Ruby-throated Hummingbirds in the eastern United States. To date, scientists have detected significant population declines in only a single North American species, the Rufous Hummingbird, but efforts are underway to monitor the health of this and other hummingbird species to help prevent them from becoming endangered.

*An elaborate garden with an array of flowers suitable for both hummingbirds and butterflies.*

*Chapter Two*

# PUTTING OUT
# THE
# WELCOME MAT

## The Basic Elements of Hummingbird Habitat

Hummingbirds are among the most welcome of all garden visitors, but many yards lack one or more of their basic requirements. Like other animals, hummingbirds need water, food, and shelter. Understanding these three elements is the first step toward creating a hummingbird haven in your yard.

Of the three basic requirements, shelter is the most critical for making hummingbirds feel at home. Hummingbirds are adapted to life in forests, woodlands, and other habitats where trees and shrubs provide suitable nest sites, refuge from aggressive rivals, and protection from predators and weather. A naturalistic landscape with a variety of cover is a proven draw for nesting, migrating, and wintering birds, while the typical suburban yard, with its vast expanse of lawn, is a virtual wasteland.

A healthy landscape also provides abundant food in the form of small insects. Though migrating hummingbirds may stop almost anywhere for a quick sip of nectar, those looking for a place to settle down have to be more selective. Insects that would not be welcome in a traditional garden, such as aphids, gnats, and fruitflies, are vital resources in the hummingbird-friendly landscape. In fact, some gardeners deliberately select plants that attract tiny insects to ensure a plentiful food supply for their avian guests. Spiders are particularly welcome, at least in spring and summer, because their silk is essential building material for nests. Pesticides are best avoided or used very sparingly to prevent upsetting the natural balance of predator and prey.

Water is perhaps the best all-around element for attracting birds in any setting, but, due to their largely liquid diet, hummingbirds need water less for drinking than for bathing. The sound of moving water is irresistible to birds, and many backyard bird specialty stores and catalogs offer drippers and misters designed to take advantage of this attraction. Decorative waterfalls and fountains are also suitable for hummingbirds, but deep basins can be hazardous to any small bird. Adding a few flat stones to create a raised platform a half-inch or less below the surface of the water will reduce the danger of drowning. To prevent transmission of diseases, any water source shared by hummingbirds and larger birds should be thoroughly cleaned at least once a week, and non-circulating pools or birdbaths should be rinsed and refilled daily.

## The Nectar Garden

Nectar plants are another vital ingredient in creating hummingbird habitat. The seemingly endless diversity of flower shape, size, and color serves to advertise different products to discriminating consumers. In the case of hummingbird-pollinated flowers, the product is abundant nectar that is rich in sucrose. This natural sugar, which most of us think of as white table sugar, is the favorite of hummingbirds and the one their favorite flowers produce in greatest abundance. Insect-pollinated flowers usually produce smaller quantities of nectar containing less desirable sugars, such as fructose and glucose. Unfortunately, when it comes to satisfying a hummingbird's tastes, many popular ornamentals, such as roses, marigolds, and geraniums, fall short in either quality or quantity of nectar. Once a hummingbird learns which flowers produce the type and amount of nectar it prefers, it seldom wastes its time on less rewarding blossoms.

The classic hummingbird-pollinated flower forms a narrow tube to fit a hummer's slender bill and exclude bees and other insects. It

*The tubular red flowers of Bee Balm (lower right corner) are more likely to attract hummingbirds than are the smaller individual flowers of the daisy family.*

23

*Bee Balms (*Monarda didyma *and relatives) are colorful and easy to grow, and they attract many hummingbirds. In some gardens they spread rapidly and may be invasive.*

has no landing platform and often points downward to further thwart potential competitors. It also has no fragrance, because like most birds hummingbirds have little or no sense of smell. Hummingbirds are particularly sensitive to colors at the warm end of the spectrum, and most of their flowers are shades of red, orange, or bright pink. This helps further reduce competition with bees and other insects, most of which don't see well in these wavelengths. However, the birds find any bright color attractive as long as it promises a sweet reward. Studies in the wild have shown that a hummingbird's "favorite" flower color varies depending on the color of the most abundant nectar source in bloom at the time. Nectar plants in shades of blue, purple, yellow, and white will add variety to your hummingbird garden.

## SELECTING PLANTS

When considering plants for your hummingbird landscape, species native to your region are the logical first choice. They are usually well adapted to local rainfall, temperatures, and soil types and are resistant to common pests and diseases. Once established, they need little or no irrigation or fertilizer. Best of all, local hummingbirds will recognize them immediately. Many native wildflowers, shrubs, and trees are now available from both mainstream and specialty nurseries, and native plant gardeners are often willing to share seeds and cuttings of favorite varieties.

*Lobelia cardinalis, the Cardinal Flower, is the archetypal hummingbird flower—bright red and tubular.*

24

A wide variety of flowers from other parts of the world will also attract hummingbirds. Many of these are pollinated by hummingbirds in Central or South America or by other birds in Africa, Asia, or Australia. Plants that are not native to your area should be selected with care to ensure that their requirements for water, sun, and soil type match your situation and that they won't take over your garden or nearby natural areas. For example, Japanese Honeysuckle (*Lonicera japonica*), though attractive to hummingbirds, is a poor choice due to its invasive habits. Also, many cultivars, including double-flowered varieties, are poor nectar producers compared to native or wild-type plants. A visit to the hummingbird garden at a nearby nature center, botanic garden, or arboretum will help you select species and varieties with the best chance of success in your landscape.

## REGIONS

Each region of the country presents unique opportunities and challenges for the hummingbird gardener. The following are general tips and plant suggestions to help you get started; local and regional resources such as state wildlife agencies, agricultural extension services, nature centers, and native plant societies can provide more specific recommendations.

*Red Columbine, Aquilegia canadensis, is colorful and easy to grow in cooler climates. Being a native, it requires little special care.*

NORTHEAST AND MIDWEST: Gardeners in this region can select from a variety of native and exotic flowers, as long as they will bloom before the birds depart in August and September. Native favorites of the Ruby-throated Hummingbird include Jewelweed (*Impatiens capensis*), Bee Balm (*Monarda didyma*), the extremely vigorous and invasive Trumpet Creeper (*Campsis radicans*), Red Columbine (*Aquilegia canadensis*), Cardinal Flower (*Lobelia cardinalis*), and Coral Honeysuckle (*Lonicera sempervirens*). Suitable non-native selections include

JEWELWEED, *IMPATIENS CAPENSIS*

Scarlet Sage (*Salvia splendens*), Texas Sage (*S. coccinea*), Four O'Clock (*Mirabilis jalapa*), Canna (*Canna indica*), Red-hot Poker (*Kniphofia uvaria*), and single varieties of Hollyhock (*Alcea rosea*). Red Buckeye (*Aesculus pavia*) and its larger cousin Horsechestnut (*A. hippocastrum*) provide both nectar and shelter.

GULF COAST AND SOUTHEAST: The warm, humid climate of this region expands the possibilities to include many subtropical species. Flowering Maple (*Abutilon pictus*), Turk's Cap (*Malvaviscus arboreus* var. *drummondii*), and other members of the mallow family do particularly well here. Red Morning Glory (*Ipomoea coccinea*), considered a weed in agricultural fields, creates a lovely cascade of tiny red trumpets as it climbs fences. Nectar sources for wintering hummingbirds include such tropicals as Firebush (*Hamelia patens*), Pineapple Sage (*Salvia elegans*), and

ROSE OF SHARON, A SHRUBBY HIBISCUS

Shrimp Plant (*Justicia brandegeana*). Evergreen Coastal Live Oaks (*Quercus virginiana*) provide year-round shelter and are visited from late summer through fall for the sap that oozes from their acorn cups.

WESTERN MOUNTAINS: The short mountain summer favors flowering shrubs and fast-growing annuals or perennials. Favorites include Skyrocket (*Ipomopsis aggregata*), columbines (*Aquilegia elegantula, triternata, chrysantha*), penstemons (*Penstemon barbatus, bridgesii*), Rocky Mountain Iris (*Iris missouriensis*), larkspurs (*Delphinium*), and Coral Bells (*Heuchera sanguinea*). Twinberry (*Lonicera involucrata*), a native shrubby honeysuckle with small red and yellow flowers, is an excellent spring nectar source, as are the manzanitas (*Arctostaphylos*). In

INDIAN PAINTBRUSH, *CASTILLEJA RHEXIFOLIA*

late summer, Rocky Mountain Bee Plant (*Cleome serrulata*) is used by southbound Calliope Hummingbirds. The various species of Indian paintbrush (*Castilleja*) can be naturalized in a wildflower meadow but are difficult to grow as garden plants. For shelter and nest sites, plant pines, spruces, or firs in the north, and pines, junipers, or evergreen oaks in the south and west.

**SOUTHWEST DESERTS:** To many gardeners, cacti are synonymous with the desert, but most native species are pollinated by insects. One hummingbird-pollinated cactus is the Claret Cup Hedgehog (*Echinocereus triglochidiatus*), found from western Texas through southern Arizona. Better plant choices for the desert hummingbird garden include penstemons (*P. barbatus, parryi, superbus*), Gregg's or Autumn Sage (*Salvia greggii*), Red Yucca (*Hesperaloe parviflora*), Ocotillo

OCOTILLO, *FOUQUIERIA SPLENDENS*

(*Fouquieria splendens*), agaves or century plants (*Agave*), chuparosas (*Justicia californica, ovata, spicigera*), desert honeysuckles (*Anisacanthus quadrifidus, thurberi*), and wolfberries (*Lycium*). Some species, such as California Fuchsia (*Zauschneria californica*), Texas Sage (*Salvia coccinea*), and Texas Betony (*Stachys coccinea*), benefit from light irrigation and afternoon shade. Hackberries (*Celtis reticulata, pallida*) provide excellent cover plus tasty fruits for other birds.

**SOUTHERN AND CENTRAL CALIFORNIA:** Gardeners in this region host hummingbirds year round, so good shelter and a wide range of nectar plants are important. Fortunately, several species of hummingbird flowers are unique to California, and many widespread western species are also common here. Red and blue larkspurs (*Delphinium*), Cardinal Monkeyflower (*Mimulus cardinalis*), Western Columbine (*Aquilegia formosa*), Red Bush Penstemon (*P. cordifolius*), California Fuchsia

CARDINAL MONKEYFLOWER, *MIMULUS CARDINALIS*

(*Zauschneria californica*), Chuparosa (*Justicia californica*), Fuchsia-flowered Gooseberry (*Ribes speciosum*), Wooly Blue Curls (*Trichostema lanatum*), and manzanitas (*Arctostaphylos*) are excellent flower choices. The birds will also take nectar from exotic plants such as citrus trees, Tree Tobacco (*Nicotiana glauca*), Bottlebrush (*Callistemon citrinus*), and various species of eucalyptus. Native evergreen oaks provide excellent shelter and nest sites.

**PACIFIC NORTHWEST:** Hummingbirds are among the most reliable pollinators in this cool, cloudy climate. Favorite native blossoms include Fireweed (*Epilobium angustifolium*), larkspurs (*Delphinium*), Red-flowering Currant (*Ribes sanguineum*), Pacific Madrone (*Arbutus menziesii*), Salmonberry (*Rubus spectabilis*), Western Columbine (*Aquilegia formosa*), Huckleberry (*Vaccinium ovatum*), and shrubby honeysuckles such as Twinberry (*Lonicera*

HARDY FUCHSIA, *FUCHSIA MAGELLANICA*

*involucrata*). A wide variety of nectar plants from other parts of North America and the world will flourish in the mild coastal climate of this region as well, including a variety of lovely fuchsias (*Fuchsia*). Conifers provide nesting sites for Rufous Hummingbirds as well as year-round shelter for Anna's Hummingbirds in coastal areas.

# Top Ten Plant Families for Hummingbird Gardens

Several groups of closely related plants stand out as nectar sources in the hummingbird garden. A few individual species are adaptable and will grow in a wide range of conditions, but each family has members suitable for a variety of growing regions.

**MINT FAMILY:** Salvias and their relatives are outstanding hummingbird plants, beautiful and easy to grow. Texas Sage (*Salvia coccinea*) and Scarlet Sage (*S. splendens*) are frost tender and usually grown as annuals. Perennials, at least in warmer climates, include Pineapple Sage (*S. elegans*), Mexican Bush Sage (*S. leucantha*), Anise Sage (*S. guaranitica*), Texas Betony (*Stachys coccinea*), Bee Balm (*Monarda didyma,*

LEMMON'S SAGE, *SALVIA LEMMONII*

*menthaefolia*), and Giant Hyssop or Hummingbird Mint (*Agastache cana, berberi*). Semi-woody species that can form sizeable shrubs include Gregg's or Autumn Sage (*S. greggii*), one of the best hummingbird plants for the Southwest, and Cleveland's Sage *(S. clevelandii*), a lovely blue-flowering species from southern California.

**HONEYSUCKLES:** Not all honeysuckles are vines, but they're all nectar-rich and many are hummingbird favorites. Trumpet or Coral Honeysuckle (*Lonicera sempervirens*), an evergreen vine with vivid orange blossoms, is an excellent choice for hummingbird gardens for most of the southern and eastern states. Unlike Japanese Honeysuckle (*L. japonica*) and other alien species, this native of the southeastern United States has not proved invasive in gardens or natural areas. Other natives include Fly Honeysuckle (*L. canadensis*), White Honeysuckle (*L. albiflora*), and Twinberry (*L. involucrata*). Hybrids such as 'Gold Flame' and 'American Beauty' are also attractive to hummingbirds.

PENSTEMONS: These stylish perennial relatives of the common snapdragon range from slender flower spikes emerging from a rosette of leaves to small shrubs covered in blossoms. Native species include Bearded Penstemon (*Penstemon barbatus*), Firecracker Penstemon (*P. eatonii*), Bridges's Penstemon *(P. bridgesii)*, Scarlet Bugler (*P. centranthifolius*), Parry's Penstemon (*P. parryi*), Arizona Penstemon *(P. pseudospectabilis*), Superb Penstemon (*P. superbus*), and Pine-needle Penstemon (*P. pinifolius*).

TURK'S CAP HIBISCUS

MALLOW FAMILY: This family includes cotton, okra, and marshmallow as well as the more familiar garden hibiscus. Native mallows that attract hummingbirds include Turk's Cap or Sultan's Turban *(Malvaviscus arboreus var. drummondii)* and Flowering Maple (*Abutilon pictus*). Also attractive to hummingbirds are single varieties of Hollyhock (*Alcea rosea*), Hardy Hibiscus (*Hibiscus moschatus*), Chinese or Tropical Hibiscus (*H. rosa-sinensis*), and Rose of Sharon (*H. syraicus*).

MORNING GLORIES: Unlike their sun-shy relatives, the tiny red flowers of the hummingbird-pollinated morning glories stay open all day for the birds' convenience. Cypress Vine (*Ipomoea quamoclit*) produces exquisite fiery red, star-shaped trumpets and is commonly available from mail-order seed companies. Red Morning Glory (*I. coccinea*) and Scarlet Creeper (*I. cristulata*) are common roadside plants in the South and Southwest and are worth cultivating at home. The perennial Bush Morning Glory (*I. leptophylla*) also draws hummingbirds to its deep pink blossoms.

SCARLET CREEPER, *IPOMOEA CRISTULATA*

*AQUILEGIA CHRYSANTHA*, A COLUMBINE

**COLUMBINES:** These elegant flowers produce their nectar at the tips of their long "spurs," where only hummingbirds and the long-tongued hawk moths can reach. A variety of red and yellow species occur throughout much of North America, including Canadian Columbine (*Aquilegia canadensis*), Barrel Columbine (*A. triternata*), Golden Columbine (*A. chrysantha*), Western Columbine (*A. formosa*), and Red Columbine (*A. elegantula*).

**BIGNONIA FAMILY:** One of the best choices for the eastern and central United States, provided you have plenty of room, is Trumpet Creeper (*Campsis radicans*). This vigorous, free-blooming deciduous vine can climb to over 50 feet in height; the 'Madame Galen' hybrid is one of several cultivars. Cross Vine (*Bignonia capreolata*) is an evergreen climber that blooms earlier than Trumpet Creeper; like its close relatives, Cross Vine spreads by underground runners as well as seed. Members of this family appropriate for the Southwest and southern California include Desert Willow (*Chilopsis linearis*) and Yellow Bells (*Tecoma stans*). Non-native Cape Honeysuckle (*Tecomaria capensis*) is also invasive and should be avoided where it might escape captivity.

*LOBELIA LAXIFLORA*

**LOBELIAS:** Brilliant scarlet blossoms are the hallmark of the most famous lobelia, Cardinal Flower (*Lobelia cardinalis*). One of the classic hummingbird flowers in the East, this species can be found in moist habitats throughout most of North America. A perennial relative, *Lobelia laxiflora*, comes from Mexico and is suited to warm southern and southwestern gardens; it bears exotic-looking red and yellow flowers on fleshy stems.

EVENING PRIMROSE FAMILY: Despite the name, this family includes several day-blooming hummingbird flowers. Fireweed (*Epilobium angustifolium*) is so named because it is among the first plants to appear after a forest fire. Its pink blossoms are a favorite with Rufous Hummingbirds in the western mountains and Pacific Northwest. Native to the Southwest, California Fuchsia (*Zauschneria californica*) bears

CALIFORNIA FUCHSIA, *ZAUSCHNERIA CALIFORNICA*

brilliant orange trumpets over pale green, velvety foliage from late summer through fall, perfect timing for southbound hummingbirds. Fuchsias (*Fuchsia*) prefer cool, humid climates, but they're worth growing wherever possible due to their beauty and attractiveness to hummingbirds.

ACANTHUS FAMILY: Some of these semi-tropical plants are adapted to humid conditions, while others are desert lovers. Desert Honeysuckle (*Anisacanthus thurberi*), Flame Acanthus (*Anisacanthus quadrifidus* var. *wrightii*), Chuparosa (*Justicia californica*), Mexican Honeysuckle (*Justicia spicigera*), and Shrimp Plant (*Justicia brandegeana*) are

*JUSTICIA OVATA*, A MEXICAN HONEYSUCKLE

popular species with both gardeners and hummingbirds.

CHUPAROSA,
*JUSTICIA CALIFORNICA*

## GARDEN LAYOUT

Though nectar plants can be incorporated into even the most formal landscapes, hummers seem most at home in casual to naturalistic gardens. In the hummingbird-friendly garden, both ornamental plants and "weeds" produce abundant crops of aphids and other insects, and there are plenty of bare twigs for sentinel perches and thick growth for hiding nests. Informal garden layouts also require less care, giving you more time to enjoy your visitors.

The ideal hummingbird garden includes a variety of nectar-rich flowers that provide continuous bloom throughout the season. For northern gardens, just three to five species of flowers may be adequate to fill this all-too-brief span, but in southern and coastal areas the season may last year round and require a much wider variety of plants. Scattering clusters of plants that bloom in different parts of the season throughout the garden will maximize feeding opportunities for multiple visitors.

Massed plantings of nectar plants are the most effective at attracting hummingbirds, and a bed of flowers in an open part of the yard will improve your chances of catching the attention of passing migrants. Nearby trees and shrubs provide perches for the birds to rest on between sips and for territorial males to keep a lookout for rivals. In windy areas, shade-loving plants can be

*Hummingbirds require shelter and perching areas, and small oak trees are excellent for this. Additionally, autumn birds sometimes feed on the sap oozing from acorn caps.*

placed under trees or at the edge of a shrub border to block the wind, making it easier for the birds to feed in gusty weather.

Even the smallest space can become a hummingbird garden. Apartment and condominium dwellers can grow nectar plants in window boxes, patio planters, and hanging baskets. Container gardening is also ideal for growing frost-tender species that must be wintered indoors. Fuchsias, bromeliads, and epiphytic cacti such

*If possible, use native plants in your hummingbird garden. Southwestern hummingbirds are familiar with and will recognize Chuparosa.*

as Christmas and Easter cacti are naturally pollinated by hummingbirds and can be used to attract birds to a balcony, deck, or patio.

## GARDEN MAINTENANCE

Most hummingbird flowers require relatively little maintenance, but a little regular care will prolong blooming and ensure next year's flower crop. Deadheading—removing spent blooms before they set fruit or seed—encourages plants to continue producing flowers. For annuals or perennials that you wish to save or share, stop deadheading a few weeks before the first frost to allow plants to set seed. Many shrubs and trees produce blooms only on new growth, so light pruning in fall or winter can help increase the number of blossoms. Pruning can also help shape and fill out young trees and shrubs planted for cover, but too much pruning may damage the plant or remove choice nesting sites.

Traditional garden maintenance includes removing dead material and killing "pests," but doing this too diligently can reduce the populations of insects that are vital to hummingbird nutrition. Even sweeping cobwebs from under the eaves is a chore best put off during hummingbird nesting season to ensure a plentiful supply of silk for building strong nests.

Pesticides are a direct danger to hummingbirds and reduce their food supply. They also destroy populations of beneficial insects. In a well-maintained garden with carefully selected plants, natural predators such as praying mantises, assassin bugs, and spiders will keep pest species in check. However, under stress from heat or drought, plants may become more susceptible to pests. In such cases, "organic" remedies such as insecticidal soap, diatomaceous earth, and pyrethrum powder are much safer than harsh chemical pesticides. Biological controls, such as *Bacillus thuringiensis* ("Bt") for caterpillars and mosquitoes as well as ladybugs or lacewings for aphids, are completely safe to use in a hummingbird garden. For serious problems where chemical treatment is necessary, applying the product after sundown will help reduce the risk to birds, bees, butterflies, and other beneficial wildlife.

*Hanging plants and hummingbird feeders go well together, but red dye in the nectar is definitely not desirable.*

*Chapter Three*

# FEEDING HUMMINGBIRDS

## Why Feeders?

Artificial feeding is a convenient, low-maintenance alternative for people with "brown thumbs" or no space for a garden, but a feeder by a window or at the edge of a deck or patio can add to your enjoyment even if your yard is a hummingbird paradise. Although feeders serve mainly to bring hummingbirds in close where they can be studied and enjoyed, properly maintained feeders may also help some birds survive when drought, late freezes, or stormy weather kills their flowers.

## Selecting a Feeder

A flower is the perfect hummingbird feeder. Its nectar supply is replenished daily and rarely lingers long enough to spoil, and each flower lasts only a few days, dropping off before it becomes infested with molds, bacteria, or other microorganisms. Artificial hummingbird feeders have a long way to go to meet these high standards, but selecting the right model can take a lot of the work and worry out of feeding hummingbirds.

Hummingbirds will drink from virtually any container as long as it contains fresh, clean sugar water, so ease of maintenance is the most important factor to consider when selecting a feeder. A clear glass or plastic reservoir is essential not only to ensure thorough cleaning but also for monitoring the liquid level. Seams, corners, and crevices are breeding grounds for the microorganisms that spoil sugar water, so the fewer of these the better.

*Yellow "bee guards" on a hummingbird feeder may actually attract bees and wasps.*

Durability is the second most important consideration. Glass is easy to clean but fragile, and the need for frequent maintenance makes broken bottles a constant hazard. Plastics resist breakage, but most types eventually become brittle when exposed to ultraviolet light, a particular problem in sunny climates and higher elevations. Better quality hummingbird feeders are made of "bullet-proof" plastics that resist sun damage; these can last ten years or more with minimal care and often come with a lifetime warranty. If you're serious about feeding hummingbirds, invest in the best quality feeder available. Though it may cost three or four times as much as a discount store model, it will pay for itself in saved replacement costs over the years.

Bees and wasps are frequent pests at hummingbird feeders, guzzling the solution and even driving the birds away. The safest and most humane way to deal with pesky flying insects is to avoid attracting them in the first place by selecting a feeder designed to resist insects. Bees and wasps can't reach as far into feeder ports as hummingbirds can, and a feeder that keeps the liquid level out of reach is likely to be ignored unless it leaks. Yellow is a popular color for insect-pollinated flowers, and while it looks attractive on a feeder it may attract unwanted attention. All-red feeders are less likely to be noticed by bees and wasps than those with yellow parts, and hummingbirds are smart enough to locate the ports without this obvious visual cue.

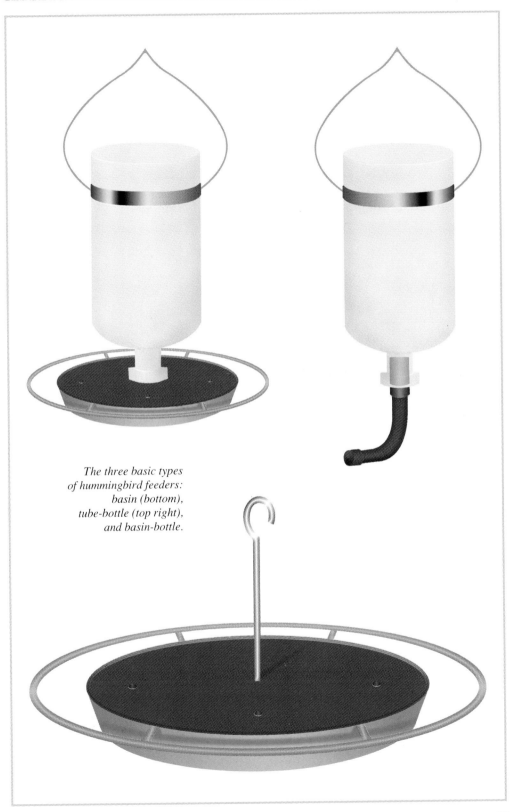

The three basic types
of hummingbird feeders:
basin (bottom),
tube-bottle (top right),
and basin-bottle.

In some parts of the country, larger birds such as finches, orioles, and woodpeckers are frequent feeder visitors. Their usual technique is to land directly on the feeder, tipping it so that the liquid runs out the ports. Many feeders can be mounted on a post using a built-in socket in the base, giving the feeders additional stability to help prevent pilferage and waste by larger birds.

Commercial feeder models range in size from 3-ounce vials ideal for a camping trip to 96-ounce monsters equivalent to thousands of flowers, but bigger isn't necessarily better where hummingbird feeders are concerned. The longer the sugar solution is out the more likely it will be to ferment and become harmful to the birds. The correct size feeder is one that holds no more solution than your local birds can drink within two or three days. Unless you live along a major flyway, a basin feeder holding between 6 and 12 ounces is the ideal choice.

To feed larger numbers of birds at a time, two or more small feeders will outperform a single large one. Except during the height of migration, one bird will typically dominate even a large feeder. Placing a second feeder a few yards away from the first will give other hummingbirds a chance to feed.

The dozens of feeder models on the market are based on three basic designs: basin, tube-bottle, and basin-bottle. The basin was the original artificial feeder. A century ago, hummingbird enthusiasts used glass jars filled with sugar water and decorated with red ribbons to attract the birds. Needless to say, modern basin feeders are far more sophisticated. This design won't leak unless broken, is easy to clean, and, unlike bottle

*A large basin-bottle feeder. Hummingbirds will come to red feeding ports and need few other attractants. Even the perches are unnecessary. Hummingbirds do not need red dye in their nectar and may acually dislike the taste of the dye.*

designs, can be refilled anytime without making a mess. You can also control the level of the solution to keep it out of reach of most insects and larger birds. Multiple ports allow several birds to feed at once. Another advantage in cooler climates or areas where hummingbirds remain all winter is that most basin-style feeders won't break if the solution freezes, unlike their bottle counterparts. The main disadvantage of basins is small capacity; this design seems to work best at volumes of 12 ounces or less.

The tube-bottle has traditionally been the most widely used type of feeder, but it has serious disadvantages. Though the bottle provides a larger reservoir than that of basin feeders, this design usually allows only one bird to feed at a time, increasing stress on feeder visitors. The narrow glass or plastic tube is

*This male Blue-throated Hummingbird is taking a drink from an advanced tube-bottle feeder.*

hard to clean and is prone to breakage. In most models, the end of the tube is covered by a red plastic or rubber tip, but if this is lost or damaged, the sharp glass edge could damage the birds' bills. The tube is usually held in place by a rubber or plastic stopper that could come loose if a larger bird perches on the tube. These feeders also drip in warm weather and can be messy to refill if not completely empty. Handcrafted versions offered at craft fairs or by mail order frequently feature pottery bottles or elaborate decorations that complicate cleaning and make it difficult to monitor the fluid level. With so many better feeders available, it's surprising that there's still a market for this design.

If you're fortunate enough to have a large hummingbird clientele, basin-bottles may be a good compromise. This design can hold more liquid on average than basin feeders and is less prone to leak than tube-bottles, though basin-bottles may drip if jarred by wind or larger birds. No basin-bottle design is as easy to clean and refill as the average basin feeder, but the added volume available to the birds will help reduce the frequency of refilling. The most practical models have pop-apart bases for thorough cleaning.

Window-mounted feeders are available in both basin and basin-bottle models. This seems like an ideal way to bring the birds in close for maximum enjoyment, but suction cup failure and ants are consistent problems with these designs. Thoroughly cleaning the window before applying the suction cup will help keep the feeder bracket on the window, and double-stick tape applied along the edge of the window may be enough to discourage ants. A simpler approach is to hang an ordinary feeder from a bracket installed above the window or from a cord, wire, or chain suspended from the eaves of the house.

## Filling the Feeder

It makes sense that the artificial nectar we use in hummingbird feeders should be as similar as possible to natural flower nectar. Pollinating insects such as bees and butterflies rely on nectar for much of their nutrition, but hummingbirds get their protein, amino acids, vitamins, minerals, and other essential nutrients from their insect prey. Nectar is mainly a source of the sugars they need to power their high-energy lifestyle, and the nectars of hummingbird flowers are little more than solutions of sugars and water.

*The primary function of a hummingbird feeder is to simulate natural feeding conditions: tubular red flowers producing nectar rich in sucrose. This is Texas Sage, Salvia coccinea.*

Not just any sugar will do to attract hummingbirds. Sucrose, better known as white table sugar, is the main ingredient in the nectar of all hummingbird-pollinated flowers. In scientifically conducted "taste tests," hummingbirds overwhelmingly preferred artificial nectars rich in sucrose to solutions containing fructose and glucose, the sugars most abundant in insect-pollinated flowers. Clearly, the plants are adapted to give their pollinators what they want and need.

Fortunately, the easiest and most economical substitute for natural nectar is also the closest to nature's own recipe. A simple, homemade solution of one part granulated white sugar in four parts ordinary tap water by volume produces a solution remarkably similar to the nectar of hummingbird flowers. The proportions need not be too precise but should fall in the range of three to five parts water to one part sugar. Weaker solutions may be ignored by the birds, and stronger ones may cause dehydration.

It is important to use only granulated white sugar. Neither powdered (confectioner's) sugar, which contains corn starch to prevent caking, nor brown sugar, which contains molasses, should be substituted for granulated sugar. Honey, though often suggested as a more healthful alternative to white sugar, should never be used in hummingbird feeders.

Besides being composed of sugars that are second-rate in attracting hummingbirds, honey contains spores that can cause fatal infections. Artificial sweeteners are another potentially dangerous substitute for white sugar. They don't provide the energy the birds need and if consumed at all could lead to starvation.

Always start with good quality water. If your tap water is cloudy or has an unpleasant taste, use bottled drinking water to mix your feeder solution. Avoid distilled or purified water, which lacks the natural mineral salts found in nectar, and chemically softened water, which may contain high levels of sodium salts. Long-term exposure to a diet containing too few or the wrong balance of salts could lead to health problems for the birds.

Though often added to commercial feeder solutions, red coloring is both unnatural and unnecessary. Flower nectar is colorless, and a small amount of red on the outside of the feeder is all that is necessary to attract the birds. Tests using dyed sugar water found that the birds preferred a colorless solution, suggesting that dyes impart an unpleasant taste. Various other additives intended to "improve" plain sugar water, such as flavorings, preservatives, and nutritional supplements, are of no real value to hummingbirds and are not recommended.

To make 12 ounces of feeder solution, enough to fill one medium or two small basin-style feeders, start with a 2-cup microwave-safe container (a glass measuring cup is perfect). Measure 1 1/3 cups water and 1/3 cup sugar into the container and stir to begin dissolving the sugar. Microwave on "high" for two to three minutes until just boiling, then remove from the oven and stir again. The heating will dissolve the sugar and kill most of the yeast and mold spores that may be lurking in the sugar or container. Always allow to cool before serving. To prevent painful and life-threatening burns to a bird's tongue, the solution should be no warmer than baby formula. If you're in a hurry to refill the feeders, dissolve the sugar in one half the total amount of boiling water, then cool with an equal amount of ice water. Leftovers can be stored in

## WHEN TO FEED

Contrary to popular folklore, leaving feeders up in fall will not prevent the birds from migrating. As with most migratory birds, instinct prompts hummingbirds to leave their nesting grounds long before their natural food supply runs out, and nothing short of captivity can dissuade a healthy hummingbird from heading south when the time comes. Unfortunately, misguided good intentions result in many feeders being taken down just as the birds are most likely to benefit from them. Tardy migrants are often young, sick, or injured, and access to a feeder may help give these disadvantaged individuals a second chance at survival.

Putting out feeders at least one week before the birds are expected to arrive in spring and leaving them out until at least one week after you've seen the last bird in fall will help ensure that no tiny traveler goes hungry. In regions where hummingbirds are not present all winter, consult your local nature center, Audubon society, or bird club for average arrival and departure dates.

Continuous feeding during the season will help establish a regular, loyal clientele. At vacation time, if feeders can't be kept clean and full by a house sitter, they should be taken down to prevent the birds from drinking spoiled solution or being frustrated by empty feeders. Hummingbirds are accustomed to short-term availability of nectar as flowers go in and out of bloom and will simply go elsewhere until you return.

a closed container in the refrigerator for up to a week. A few minutes at room temperature or a few seconds in the microwave will warm the solution to a safe serving temperature.

Once you get an idea of how much sugar water the birds are drinking, it may be more practical to make up to a week's worth at a time and store it in the refrigerator. Larger quantities are more easily made using water boiled on the stove top. Measure the water after boiling to ensure correct proportions.

## Feeder Maintenance

Sugar water is much more perishable than seed, and hummingbird feeders should be rinsed and refilled regularly even if the birds are not emptying them. Ideally, the amount of solution available, whether in one feeder or many, should last no more than two to three days. Starting out with a small amount of solution until you learn how much the birds are using will minimize both work and waste. Discarded sugar water isn't just money down the drain; every acre of sugar cane or sugar beets equals one less acre of habitat for hummingbirds and other wildlife plus tons of pesticides and other pollutants added to our environment.

Feeders should be thoroughly cleaned at least once a week, though rinsing with hot water before refilling will delay the growth of molds, yeasts, and bacteria. If you own just one feeder, performing this chore at night will minimize the time the birds

*A selection of sturdy, serviceable hummingbird feeders.*

must do without. Duplicate feeders can be a time-saver; one set can be inside being cleaned and refilled while the other is in use.

Feeders can be cleaned safely and effectively in a solution of one part vinegar to about five parts hot water. Persistent problems with fermentation or stubborn accumulations of mold usually respond to soaking in a solution of one part chlorine bleach to ten parts hot water. Some feeder manufacturers have created brushes and mops especially for hard-to-clean feeders, but table or rock salt is equally useful. One or two tablespoons of salt mixed with an equal amount of water and swirled vigorously inside the feeder will scour off mold and other contaminants without harming the feeder; the debris and remaining salt will rinse away easily. Dishwashing detergent should be used with care to avoid leaving a residue. No matter which cleaner you use, always rinse the feeder well before refilling.

*A captive Rufous Hummingbird feeding from a tube-bottle feeder with a large bee guard. Captive hummingbirds are given a fortified nectar mix to make up for the absence of insects in their diet.*

## Feeder Troubleshooting

The most common problems with hummingbird feeders involve uninvited guests. Ants are astonishingly resourceful at finding feeders, and the only sure way to discourage them is with a barrier. Commercial ant barriers that hang between the feeder and its support come in two basic designs. Ant moats, which must be kept full of water, require the most maintenance; this feature is built into some feeder models. More convenient are maintenance-free barriers that incorporate a greasy or tacky substance inside an inverted cup where the birds won't come into contact with it. It may be tempting simply to smear the exposed hanging wire or the feeder itself with cooking oil, petroleum jelly, or a sticky insect barrier product such as "Tree Tanglefoot," but this is dangerous. Each year wildlife rehabilitators take in dozens of hummingbirds whose wings have become matted with greasy or gummy materials, and some of these birds don't survive to be released.

*A simple ant barrier can be made by affixing a spray can cap on a length of electrical conduit on which a feeder is mounted. Fill with petroleum jelly as an insect barrier.*

For post-mounted feeders, a short length of double-stick tape wrapped around the post a few inches from the bottom forms an inexpensive but temporary ant barrier. A more permanent barrier can be made from a discarded spray can cap. Select a cap in a neutral color to avoid confusing the birds. In the top center of the cap, cut or drill a hole just large enough to slide the post through. Orient the cap upside down to use as a water-filled moat or right side up to use with petroleum jelly or an insect barrier product. Secure the cap to the post a foot or more from the ground with silicone or latex caulking.

Bees and wasps present a much greater challenge. One common attractant is sugar water splashed or dripped on the outside of the feeder during refilling. It takes only a few drops to attract these insects, so clean up spills promptly and thoroughly. If the feeder has been carefully selected for insect resistance, the problem may be a damaged port or leaky seal. Insects gathering around just one part of the feeder, especially if it's away from any port, usually indicate a crack or seam failure in that area. For persistent problems, some people put out shallow dishes of sugar water to draw bees and

*Paper wasps and other hymenopterans will be attracted to any spills or leaks from a feeder. They also are attracted to the color yellow.*

wasps away from the feeders, but this ultimately results in attracting more bees to the yard and increasing their population. Wasp traps baited with both meat and spoiled feeder solution will attract and kill yellowjackets, hornets, paper wasps, and honeybees without resorting to pesticides. These traps are available at garden centers and hardware stores.

*Orioles (here a Baltimore Oriole) come to feeders for oranges and other fruit and think nothing of banging about a hummingbird feeder until the sugar water splashes out. If you have this problem, avoid perches and securely fix the feeder onto a post.*

Larger birds such as woodpeckers, orioles, and finches can be a nuisance, frightening the hummingbirds away, spilling more sugar water than they drink, and contaminating the feeder with their droppings. They can often be lured away with open containers of sugar water, but this may lead to bee problems. Feeders without perches sometimes discourage these freeloaders; some models have optional perches, while others have none at all. If the problem persists, the most effective solution is to mount the feeder on a post, which will also prevent the sugar water from sloshing out in windy weather. Several models have a post socket molded into the bottom for convenience. A 6-foot length of 3/8-inch electrical conduit sunk at least one foot into the ground for stability makes an inexpensive feeder post that can also be used for seed feeders in winter. For more permanent installation, set the feeder post in concrete as you would a fence post.

The list of feeder visitors also includes some mammals. Squirrels, raccoons, opossums, and ringtails are adept climbers and can damage as well as drain feeders. Hanging the feeder under a dome or disk designed to discourage squirrels may help. Bears can be a problem in some areas; bringing the feeder in at night or rigging a pulley system to keep it out of reach is often the only effective means of discouraging them. In the desert Southwest, three species of nectar-drinking bats, including one endangered species, have learned to visit hummingbird feeders to supplement their natural diet of cactus and agave nectar. These fascinating and harmless animals are worth hosting but often drain feeders nightly during their late summer migration. Rather than bringing feeders in at night or refilling them at dawn, some residents of nectar bat country place their feeders inside cylindrical cages made from 4-inch by 6-inch fence wire.

*Hummingbird gardens provide flowers for feeding, cover for safety, and small insects and spiders for food.*

*Chapter Four*

# PROVIDING A
# SAFE HAVEN

No one who loves hummingbirds enough to attract them to their yard would deliberately put them in harm's way, but some aspects of our human environment that we take for granted pose serious threats to the birds' survival. Pesticides are an excellent example. Just as antibiotics can upset the body's populations of beneficial microorganisms, insecticides, herbicides, fungicides, and other garden chemicals can disrupt or destroy the complex natural community your garden visitors depend on. Poisons intended for pests will also kill birds, lizards, frogs, beneficial insects, spiders, and other

*Because they slow down to investigate window-mounted feeders, hummingbirds seldom crash into windows at full speed and thus avoid injury.*

small animals as well as the insects they feed on, resulting in increased pest problems in the long run.

No matter how responsible your own gardening practices are, your yard and its wildlife can be affected by the thoughtless actions of others. Even totally organic gardens may be contaminated by careless application of pesticides on neighboring properties, and hummingbirds and other wildlife can be poisoned when they feed in these chemically-treated landscapes. Encouraging your neighbors and community to use non-toxic pest control methods such as barriers, repellents, and biological controls in place of chemical pesticides is an important step toward a healthier environment for both people and wildlife.

Concentrations of birds around feeders sometimes attract the attention of wild predators. Small hawks and owls, large flycatchers, roadrunners, and praying mantises occasionally eat adult hummingbirds, but not enough to affect populations. Their presence is one sign of a healthy backyard ecosystem. Cats, on the other hand, are an unnatural and increasing threat to wildlife, including hummingbirds. Scientists estimate that free-roaming domestic cats, even well-fed pets, kill hundreds of millions of birds and other small animals each year. Hummingbirds are a tempting target, and some cats become adept at swatting them out of the air as they approach feeders. Birds have little immunity to the bacteria in cats' mouths, and survivors of such attacks often die later from infection.

But protecting wildlife isn't the only reason to keep cats indoors. Cars, dogs, coyotes, poisons, traps, diseases, and parasites are a few of the hazards that await free-roaming cats. Studies have shown that indoor-only cats have a life expectancy up to four times longer than those allowed outdoors. Cats also raid garbage cans and foul flower beds and playgrounds with their droppings, putting both people and other pets at risk for disease. The Humane Society of the United States and the American Humane Association have joined the American Bird Conservancy in a campaign to encourage cat owners to protect pets, wildlife, and public health by keeping cats indoors.

Where cats are a problem, a few precautions will help save birds' lives. Feeders should be placed at least 5 feet off the ground and far enough from windowsills and fences to keep visiting birds out of striking distance. Low bushes near feeders should be trimmed up to eliminate hiding places for cats waiting in ambush. Contrary to popular belief, belling a cat does not reduce kills; research has shown that the stealthy felines quickly learn to compensate for this handicap. If none of these methods eliminates the problem, contact your local humane society, cat rescue organization, or animal control agency about renting or borrowing a humane trap.

Windows can be deadly to birds, but hummingbirds seem less prone to such accidents than many songbirds. Their quick reflexes and maneuverability may help them avoid collisions, but battles occasionally result in one of the combatants flying headlong into glass. Hanging feeders or baskets of flowers directly in front of windows may actually help prevent window kills by reducing the likelihood of a high-speed impact and familiarizing the birds with the presence of the glass. Other methods of reducing window kills include hanging strips of cloth or aluminum foil, orchard netting, or weighted strands of monofilament fishing line in front of the window.

Despite your best efforts to provide a safe haven for hummingbirds, accidents can still happen. If you find an injured or sick hummingbird, contact your local nature center, zoo, or state wildlife agency office immediately for the name of a licensed wildlife rehabilitator or wildlife care center near you. The care and rehabilitation of injured wildlife are best left to experts, and federal law prohibits possession of native birds and their eggs, nests, or feathers without a permit.

*Cats will quickly learn where feeders are placed and will stalk birds from any nearby hiding places. Make sure all feeders are far enough from the ground, surfaces cats can jump from, and potential hiding places if you wish to avoid cat predation on hummers and other birds.*

*A male Black-chinned Hummingbird at a colorful feeder.*

*Chapter Five*

# SHARING THE GIFT OF HUMMINGBIRDS

Nature truly is the gift that keeps on giving. Sharing your love of hummingbirds with neighbors, friends, and relatives can enrich their lives and broaden appreciation and protection of our natural world. Instead of another toy, neck tie, or bottle of cologne, giving that special person a hummingbird feeder, packets of flower seeds, and a copy of this guide may be the beginning of a lifelong love affair with nature.

Many traditional gardeners are unaware of the rewards of landscaping for wildlife. Take photos of your garden and its visitors and share them at garden club meetings or on your personal web site, along with

*Many nature centers today have colorful butterfly and hummingbird gardens designed to attract both types of animals and appeal to a variety of observers.*

a list of plants and tips for a successful hummingbird garden. Offer seeds and cuttings from your favorite hummingbird flowers to fellow gardeners. Patronize nurseries that stock native plants favored by hummingbirds, butterflies, and other welcome garden visitors, and encourage other businesses to follow their example.

The lessons you learn in your own garden can be applied to community projects. Botanic gardens and nature centers often have demonstration bird and butterfly gardens where volunteers plant, water, and weed, as well as give public and school tours. Many schools have involved students in creating gardens for hummingbirds, butterflies, and other wildlife, and health care professionals have begun to recognize the healing value of nature. A school, hospital, or nursing home near you may appreciate assistance with a hummingbird garden project.

To ensure a future for hummingbirds and other migratory birds, support local and international efforts to protect nesting and wintering habitat and migratory stopover sites. Let your local, state, and national representatives know that hummingbirds, warblers, orioles, tanagers, thrushes, and others are an irreplaceable part of our natural heritage and that you care about their future. Get involved with grassroots organizations dedicated to the welfare of birds and their habitat.

Recycling household waste and using recycled and environmentally friendly products are important steps toward ensuring future abundance of the natural resources that birds and humans alike need to survive. Composting garden and kitchen wastes saves space in landfills and supplies additional food for hummingbirds in the form of small insects. Even choosing the right kind of coffee can have a positive impact on wintering habitat for migratory birds. Agriculture is the greatest threat to hummingbird habitat in the tropics, but coffee is one crop that can be grown with limited impact on birds and their environment. Birds thrive in organic shade coffee plantations, and the demand for premium shade-grown coffees has helped save thousands of acres of bird habitat from conversion to sterile fields of sun-grown varieties. Other "bird-friendly" products are beginning to appear on store shelves, including organically grown bananas and sustainably harvested wood products.

*A male Anna's Hummingbird at a simple tube-bottle feeder.*

*A female Broad-tailed Hummingbird feeding on thistle.*

*Chapter Six*

# A GUIDE TO HUMMINGBIRDS

## OF THE UNITED STATES AND CANADA

Hummingbird identification is more challenging than most people realize. Adult male hummingbirds are usually best identified by the color and shape of their gorgets, the brilliantly iridescent areas on their throats. Females and immature males show more subtle colors and patterns on the throat, but these are often just as important. The color, shape, and pattern of the outer three pairs of tail feathers are useful in sorting out birds of both sexes and all ages. Back color is generally not very helpful; except for some adult male Rufous, all hummingbirds found in the United States and Canada have some shade of green on their backs. A field guide to North American birds can help you sort out the differences.

### RUBY-THROATED HUMMINGBIRD

**Size:** 3 3/4"

**Adult Male:** ruby-red throat with a narrow black chin strap, contrasting with white upper breast; outer tail feathers black, pointed

**Female:** small, pale gray below and bright green above; bill is medium length and straight to slightly curved; slightly rounded outer tail feathers are banded in gray-green, black, and white

**Range:** common summer resident from eastern Texas and Oklahoma east to Atlantic Coast, north to Labrador, and west to Saskatchewan

**Habitat:** forest and woodland

**Nesting Season:** late spring through summer

**Migration:** arrives on breeding grounds in spring, leaves in late summer or fall to winter in Mexico and Central America; occasionally wanders west during migration

### BLACK-CHINNED HUMMINGBIRD

**Size:** 3 3/4"

**Adult Male:** velvety black gorget with a violet band at the bottom, contrasting with white upper breast; outer tail feathers black and pointed

**Female:** small, pale gray below and dull to moderately bright green above, with a dingy grayish crown; bill is long and slightly curved; rounded to pointed outer tail feathers are banded in gray-green, black, and white

**Range:** common to abundant summer resident from central Texas and Oklahoma west to California and northwestern Mexico, north to southern British Columbia

**Habitat:** woodland, streamside forest and desert scrub

**Nesting Season:** late spring through summer

**Migration:** arrives on breeding grounds in spring, leaves in late summer or fall to winter in western and southern Mexico; occasionally wanders east during migration and winters along Gulf Coast

### ANNA'S HUMMINGBIRD

**Size:** 4"

**Adult Male:** both gorget and crown are rose red to coppery red, upper breast is dull gray; outer tail feathers are gray and blunt-tipped

**Female:** medium-sized, dull to bright green above and grayish below; bill is medium length and straight; rounded outer tail feathers are banded in gray, black, and white; adult female usually has an irregular patch of iridescent red in the center of the throat

**Range:** common to abundant year-round resident from California east to far western Texas, north to southern British Columbia

**Habitat:** woodland, chaparral, urban, and suburban areas

**Nesting Season:** late winter through spring

**Migration:** mostly resident, wanders south and into the mountains in summer and fall

## COSTA'S HUMMINGBIRD

**Size:** 3 1/2"

**Adult Male:** violet to purple gorget with extremely long extensions, crown the same color; narrow, pointed outer tail feathers are medium gray

**Female:** very small, with pale gray underparts and dull to bright green back; may have a small blackish or iridescent purple spot in center of throat; bill is very short and thin; tail is very short, with rounded outer feathers banded in gray, black, and white

**Range:** common year-round resident in southern California east to southern Arizona and south to northwestern Mexico, summer resident north to central California, southern Nevada, and Utah

**Habitat:** desert scrub, chaparral, and suburban areas

**Nesting Season:** late winter through spring

**Migration:** arrives on breeding grounds in late winter to early spring, wanders south or to higher elevations in summer and fall

## RUFOUS HUMMINGBIRD

**Size:** 3 3/4"

**Adult Male:** red-orange to yellow-orange gorget, contrasting with white upper breast; back bright rufous, often with large patches of green; long, pointed tail feathers are rufous with black tips

**Female:** small, bright rufous and cream below and bright green above, usually with iridescent red-orange patch in center of throat; bill is short and thin; tail is medium-length to long, with blunt-tipped outer feathers boldly banded in rufous, black, and white

**Range:** common spring and summer resident from the northern border of California to southeastern Alaska, east to western Montana

**Habitat:** coniferous forest

**Nesting Season:** late spring through summer

**Migration:** arrives on breeding grounds in late winter to early spring, leaves as early as June (adult males) for wintering grounds in western and southern Mexico; common migrant along Pacific Coast and through the western mountains; some individuals wander east during migration to winter in Southeast and along Gulf Coast, rare elsewhere in the East in fall and winter

## ALLEN'S HUMMINGBIRD

**Size:** 3 3/4"

**Adult Male:** like male Rufous Hummingbird except upper back is bright green; lower back may be entirely rufous or mixed with green; tail feathers are rufous with black tips, outer pair extremely narrow and pointed

**Female:** like female Rufous Hummingbird

**Range:** Common spring and summer resident along the Pacific Coast from southern California to southern Oregon; permanent resident on the Palos Verdes Peninsula and nearby coastal islands of southern California.

**Habitat:** chaparral and woodland

**Nesting Season:** late winter through summer

**Migration:** arrives on breeding grounds in late winter to early spring, leaves by late summer for wintering grounds in south-central Mexico, except for non-migratory population in southern California; may wander east during migration to winter along Gulf Coast

## BROAD-TAILED HUMMINGBIRD

**Size:** 4"

**Adult Male:** rose red to hot pink gorget, contrasting with white upper breast; crown and back bright green; central tail feathers are pointed, blunt outer feathers are black with narrow rufous edging

**Female:** medium-sized, pale rufous and white below and bright green above, with a white to pale cream throat delicately spangled with bronze green; bill is medium length and thin; outer feathers of the long pointed tail are banded with rufous, black, and white

**Range:** Common to abundant summer resident of western mountains from southern Arizona and far western Texas to Idaho and Wyoming; year-round resident in mountains from northern Mexico to Guatemala

**Habitat:** coniferous forest and mountain meadows

**Nesting Season:** summer

**Migration:** arrives on breeding grounds in late winter or early spring, leaves by early fall for wintering grounds in western and southern Mexico; occasionally wanders east to winter along Gulf Coast

## CALLIOPE HUMMINGBIRD

FEMALE

**Size:** 3 1/4"

**Adult Male:** gorget of wine red streaks over white background, contrasting with white upper breast; back is bright green; bill is very short and thin; tail is very short and notched, outer feathers are gray and rounded

**Female:** very small, with pale rufous and white below and bright green above; pale cream to white throat is delicately spangled with bronze green; bill is very short and thin; very short and slightly notched tail, with rounded outer feathers banded in gray, black, and white, usually with a small amount of rufous

**Range:** Uncommon summer resident of western mountains from northern Baja California north to central British Columbia, east to Wyoming, Montana and western Alberta

**Habitat:** coniferous forest and mountain meadows

**Nesting Season:** summer

**Migration:** arrives on breeding grounds in spring, leaves by late summer for wintering grounds in western and southern Mexico; occasionally wanders east to winter along Gulf Coast

MALE

## BUFF-BELLIED HUMMINGBIRD

**Size:** 4 1/4"

**Male and Female:** large, with bright green head, chest, and back (no distinct gorget); buff or tan belly; long red bill with black tip; entire tail is bright rufous with green highlights

**Range:** uncommon summer or year-round resident in lower Rio Grande Valley and along southern Gulf Coast of Texas south to Central America; rare winter resident along northern Gulf Coast

**Habitat:** coastal scrub and woodland

**Nesting Season:** spring through summer

**Migration:** most individuals resident; after breeding season some move north to winter in central Gulf Coast region

## BROAD-BILLED HUMMINGBIRD

**Size:** 4"

**Adult Male:** cobalt blue throat blends into deep green of breast, upper belly, and back; lower belly and undertail coverts are pale to medium gray; long red bill with black tip; tail is steel blue with dark gray edges on central feathers

**Female:** medium-sized, with plain pale to medium gray throat and underparts and a pale line behind the eye contrasting with a dark stripe below; back and crown are deep green; long bill is black with red-orange at base; rounded outer tail feathers are blue-black with white tips

**Range:** common but local summer resident of southeastern Arizona and northwestern Mexico, year-round resident of central Mexico; rare in summer in southwestern New Mexico and far western Texas, occasionally wanders

**Habitat:** desert scrub and woodlands

**Nesting Season:** spring through summer

**Migration:** most individuals leave breeding range by October to winter in western Mexico; a few remain in Arizona all year or wander east or west in fall

## LUCIFER HUMMINGBIRD

**Size:** 3 3/4"

**Adult Male:** brilliant magenta to violet gorget, contrasting with white upper breast and sides of neck; bill is long and distinctly curved; tail is long, narrow, and deeply forked

**Female:** small, pale rusty below and bright green above, with plain throat and a dark, curving line behind the eye; bill is long and distinctly curved; tail is long, very narrow, with outer feathers banded in rufous, black, and white

**Range:** rare to uncommon summer resident from western Texas, southern New Mexico, and southeastern Arizona to northern Mexico; year-round resident in central and southern Mexico

**Habitat:** desert scrub and mountain woodlands

**Nesting Season:** late spring through summer

**Migration:** arrives on breeding grounds in April, leaves by early fall to winter in western Mexico

## MAGNIFICENT HUMMINGBIRD

**Size:** 5 1/4"

**Adult Male:** very large, with bright green gorget and purple to violet crown; breast is black with bronze-green highlights, back is dark green; gray undertail coverts contrast with dark bronze-green notched tail

**Female:** very large, with medium gray throat and underparts and dark green back; white spot and uneven pale stripe behind eye contrast with dark cheek stripe; bill is very long and all black; outer tail feathers are banded in bronze-green, black, and grayish white

**Range:** common summer resident in mountains of southeastern Arizona, southwestern New Mexico, and western Texas; year-round resident from western Mexico to Central America; rarely wanders north or east in fall

**Habitat:** coniferous forest and oak woodland in mountain canyons

**Nesting Season:** late spring through summer

**Migration:** most individuals leave breeding range by October to winter in western Mexico; a few are resident around feeders in southeastern Arizona

## BLUE-THROATED HUMMINGBIRD

**Size:** 5 1/4"

**Adult Male:** very large, with bright blue gorget, uniformly gray breast and belly; bold face pattern includes white stripe behind eye, dark gray cheek, and narrow white streak along jaw line; crown and shoulders are bright green, back is bronze green blending to blackish rump; entire tail is blue-black with large white spots on outer feathers

**Female:** similar to male but with gray throat

**Range:** uncommon and local summer resident in mountains of southeastern Arizona, southern New Mexico, and western Texas; year-round resident in mountains of Mexico; rarely wanders north or east in fall

**Habitat:** streamside forests in mountain canyons

**Nesting Season:** late spring through summer.

**Migration:** most individuals leave breeding range by October to winter in western Mexico; a few are resident around feeders in southeastern Arizona

## VIOLET-CROWNED HUMMINGBIRD

**Size:** 4 1/2"

**Male and Female:** large, with entirely snow-white underparts, bright blue-violet crown, red bill with black tip; back and tail dull gray-green

**Range:** uncommon and local summer resident of southeastern Arizona, southwestern New Mexico; year-round resident in western Mexico; visitor to western Texas and California

**Habitat:** cottonwood and sycamore forest along desert and canyon streams

**Nesting Season:** summer through early fall

**Migration:** most individuals leave breeding range by late fall to winter in western Mexico; a few winter in Arizona

# Tropical Hummingbirds That Occasionally Visit the United States and Canada

WHITE-EAR

**WHITE-EARED HUMMINGBIRD:** rare summer resident of mountain canyons in southeastern Arizona; visitor to New Mexico, western Texas, and the Gulf Coast; bold white eye stripe, black cheek, grayish white belly, bronze-green tail, and short red and black bill are distinctive.

**BERYLLINE HUMMINGBIRD:** rare summer resident in the mountain canyons of southeastern Arizona; visitor to New Mexico and western Texas; similar to Buff-bellied Hummingbird, but with more green on breast, darker belly, and dark rust-brown tail glossed with purple iridescence.

**GREEN VIOLET-EAR:** rare visitor to the eastern and central states from central Mexico; very large, dark green, with blue-violet patches on cheek and breast.

**PLAIN-CAPPED STARTHROAT:** rare visitor to southern Arizona from western Mexico; very large, with a very long bill, short tail, bold white facial stripes, and a patch of white in the center of the rump.

**BAHAMA WOODSTAR:** rare visitor to Florida from the Bahamas; male has rose-red gorget and deeply forked tail, female's tail is banded in green, black, and rufous.

**CUBAN EMERALD:** very rare visitor to Florida from Cuba; male is entirely green on back, throat, breast, and belly, female is grayish white below; both sexes have forked tail.

**CINNAMON HUMMINGBIRD:** very rare visitor to Arizona and New Mexico from Mexico; like Buff-bellied Hummingbird, but underparts are entirely cinnamon-colored.

**GREEN-BREASTED MANGO:** very rare visitor to the Gulf Coast from eastern Mexico; large, with distinctly curved bill; male is entirely dark green to blue below, female has broad dark stripe down center of white breast and belly.

**XANTUS'S HUMMINGBIRD:** very rare visitor to the Pacific Coast from Baja California; like White-eared Hummingbird but with cinnamon belly, rust and green tail.

## A SIX-LEGGED HUMMINGBIRD?

If you think you've seen the world's smallest hummingbird, look again. It may be one of many species of sphinx or hawk moths. These large-bodied insects look and act so much like hummingbirds that at a distance or in dim light it's easy to overlook the six thin legs and pair of short antennae. Unlike most moths, sphinx moths are often active in broad daylight, hovering in front of flowers to sip nectar through long, beak-like tongues. A thick coat of fur-like scales looks remarkably like feathers and serves to keep the insect's body temperature high for maximum flight efficiency. The larvae of these moths are commonly known as hornworms; though some feed on crops such as tomatoes and tobacco, most are harmless links in the food chain.

*Sphinx moths, such as this Titan Sphinx photographed in southern Arizona, often are mistaken for hummingbirds. Look for the antennae!*

# RESOURCES

## Organizations

### THE HUMMINGBIRD SOCIETY
P.O. Box 394
Newark, DE 19715
(800) 529-3699
http://www.hummingbird.org
A non-profit organization dedicated to international understanding and conservation of hummingbirds.

### AMERICAN BIRD CONSERVANCY
1250 24th Street NW, Suite 400
Washington, DC 20037
(202) 778-9666
http://www.abcbirds.org
A non-profit organization dedicated to preserving the unique bird life of the Americas, including neotropical migrants such as hummingbirds.

### CAPE MAY BIRD OBSERVATORY
Center for Research and Education
600 Route 47 North
Cape May Court House, NJ 08210
(609) 861-0700
http://www.njas.org/abtnjas/abtnjas/cmbo.html
One of several education centers of the New Jersey Audubon Society. Staff and volunteer naturalists offer walks, workshops, and other activities year round, including hummingbird walks in late summer and early fall. Center features demonstration gardens for hummingbirds, butterflies, etc.; hummingbird flowers and other wildlife-friendly plants available for purchase spring through fall.

### SOUTHEASTERN ARIZONA BIRD OBSERVATORY
P.O. Box 5521
Bisbee, AZ 85603-5521
(520) 432-1388
http://www.sabo.org
A non-profit organization dedicated to conservation of the birds of southeastern Arizona. Offers field trips, workshops, and other activities year round, including hummingbird programs in late summer. Hummingbird banding project on the San Pedro River (spring and summer) is open to the public. Web site includes frequently asked questions about hummingbirds, photo feature on hummingbird banding, links to books and other resources.

### HUMMER/BIRD STUDY GROUP
P.O. Box 250
Clay, AL 35048-0250
(205) 681-2888
http://www.hbsg.org
A non-profit organization dedicated to the study and preservation of hummingbirds and other neotropical migrants in the Southeast. Conducts research and educational activities; migration banding station at Fort Morgan, Alabama, is open to visitors.

### LADY BIRD JOHNSON WILDFLOWER CENTER
(formerly National Wildflower Research Center)
4801 La Crosse Avenue
Austin, TX 78739
(512) 292-4200
http://www.wildflower.org
A non-profit organization founded by the former First Lady to educate people about the environmental necessity, economic value, and natural beauty of our native plants. Offers educational activities and publications and acts as a clearinghouse for information on sources for wildflower seed and nursery stock.

## Web Resources
(except those listed under "Organizations")

### HUMMINGBIRDS!
http://www.hummingbirds.net
A little bit of everything about hummingbirds, including species profiles, frequently asked questions, migration maps, product reviews, reprints of scientific papers, and an extensive bibliography. Designed and maintained by Lanny Chambers.

### NATIONAL AUDUBON SOCIETY
http://www.audubon.org
General information on this national conservation organization plus contact information for local chapters throughout the United States.

## Books and Videos

### THE HUMMINGBIRD BOOK
by Donald and Lillian Stokes
Little Brown & Co. 1989
A colorful beginner's guide to attracting, feeding and identifying the hummingbirds of North America.

### A FIELD GUIDE TO HUMMINGBIRDS
by Sheri Williamson
Houghton Mifflin Co. 2001
An in-depth guide to field identification of every species of hummingbird found north of Mexico, illustrated with color photos.

### HUMMINGBIRDS: THE SUN CATCHERS
by Jeff and April Sayre
NorthWord Press 1996
The amazing lives of hummingbirds plus profiles of North American species, illustrated with beautiful photos.

### HUMMINGBIRDS: JEWELS IN FLIGHT
by Connie Toops
Voyageur Press 1992
Hummingbird behavior and natural history interspersed with personal accounts of the author's travels in search of hummingbirds.

### RUBY-THROATED HUMMINGBIRD
by Robert Sargent
Stackpole Books 1999
An in-depth look at the life of the most familiar of North American hummingbirds, by a prominent hummingbird bander and founder of the Hummer/Bird Study Group.

### HUMMINGBIRD GARDENS: ATTRACTING NATURE'S JEWELS TO YOUR BACKYARD
by Nancy L. Newfield and Barbara Neilsen
Houghton Mifflin Co. 1996
Real-life examples of successful backyard hummingbird habitats in six major regions of the United States and Canada, with sample garden layouts and extensive lists of hummingbird-friendly plants for each region.

### WILDLIFE VIEWING GUIDES
published by Falcon Press
A unique, multi-agency project developed in cooperation with Defenders of Wildlife, this series of concise travel guides will direct you to the best wildlife viewing areas in each state, including hummingbird hotspots.

### A BIRDER'S GUIDE TO SOUTHEASTERN ARIZONA
by Richard Cachor Taylor
American Birding Association 1995 (updated 1999)
The best resource for planning a visit to this hummingbird-lover's paradise.

### THE WORLD OF THE HUMMINGBIRD
by Harry Thurston
Sierra Club Books 1999
A poet and award-winning author explores the lives and travels of some of North America's most remarkable birds.

### WATCHING HUMMINGBIRDS
Nature Science Network
The lives and behavior of hummingbirds,, including courtship, nesting, and territoriality.

## Magazines

### WILDBIRD
Subscription Department
P.O. Box 52898
Boulder, CO 80323-2898
This full-sized magazine features colorful articles, photo features, and an annual hummingbird issue (May).

### BIRD WATCHER'S DIGEST
P.O. Box 110
Marietta, OH 45750
(800) 879-2473
Though small in format (the size of Reader's Digest), BWD is packed with articles and feature columns by some of America's best-known birders.

### BIRDS & BLOOMS
P.O. Box 5359
Harlan, IA 51593-0859
http://www.reimanpub.com/Magazines/BB/BBPage.html
A colorful advertising-free magazine for gardeners who love birds, butterflies, and other wildlife.

## Acknowledgments
My sincerest thanks to my husband and colleague Tom Wood for his wise counsel and loving support; to the many passionate and knowledgeable participants in the Humnet discussion group, especially Van Remsen, Lanny Chambers, Bob Sargent, and Nancy Newfield; to Hummingbird Society founder Ross Hawkins for recommending me to T.F.H. for this project; and, last but not least, to the birds for their endless inspiration.

# INDEX

Page numbers in **bold** indicate photos

Acanthus family, 31
Allen's Hummingbird, **57**
   identification of, 57
Anna's Hummingbird, **15**, **18**, **53**, **56**
   identification of, 56
Bahama Woodstar,
   identification of, 61
Bee Balms, *Monarda*, **23**, **24**
Bee guards, 36, **36**, **43**
Berylline Hummingbird,
   identification of, 60
Bignonia family, 30
Birds, as feeder pests, 45
Black-chinned Hummingbird,
   **14**, **17**, **51**, **56**
   identification of, 56
Blue-throated Hummingbird,
   **39**, **60**
   identification of, 60
Broad-billed Hummingbird, **4**, **59**
   identification of, 59
Broad-tailed Hummingbird, **13**, **54**, **58**
   identification of, 58
Buff-bellied Hummingbird,
   identification of, 58
California Fuchsia,
   *Zauschneria*, **31**
Calliope Hummingbird, **58**
   identification of, 58
Cardinal Flower, *Lobelia*, **24**, 30, **30**, **40**
Cats, as pests, 48-49, **49**
Chicks, 17-18
Chuparosa, *Justicia*, **31**, **33**
Cinnamon Hummingbird,
   identification of, 61
Colors, 8
Columbines, *Aquilegia*, **25**, 30, **30**
Costa's Hummingbird, **6**, **16**, **57**
   identification of, 57
Courtship, 16-17
Cuban Emerald, identification of, 61
Enemies and dangers, 19
Evening primrose family, 31

Feeder maintenance, 42-43
Feeder pests, 43-45
Feeders, 36-40
   types of, **37**
Flight, 6
Flowers, dependence on, 13-14
Garden & feeder safety, 47-49
Garden layout & maintenance, 32-33
Gopher Snake, *Pituophis*, **19**
Green Violet-ear, identification of, 60
Green-breasted Mango,
   identification of, 61
Green-crowned Brilliant, **9**
Growth, 17-18
Habitat requirements, 21ff
Hardy Fuchsia, *Fuchsia*, **27**
Hawk moths, 61, **61**
Hibiscus, *Hibiscus*, **29**
Honeysuckles, 28
Hummingbird identification, 55-61
Identification of U.S.
   hummingbirds, 55-61
Indian Paintbrush, *Castilleja*, **26**
Insects, as food, 14
Insects, as pests, 43-44
Intelligence, 7-8
Jewel Weed, *Impatiens*, **26**
Life span, 19
Lobelias, 30
Lucifer Hummingbird, **59**
   identification of, 59
Magnificent Hummingbird, **59**
   identification of, 59
Mallow family, 29
Mammals, as feeder pests, 45
Mexican Honeysuckles,
   *Justicia*, **31**
Migrations, 11-13
Mint family, 28
Monkeyflower, *Mimulus*, **27**
Morning Glories, 29
Morning Glories, *Ipomoea*, **29**
Nectar, 6, 14, 40
Nectar for feeders, 40-42
Nectar gardens, 22ff

Nectar plants, 24ff
Nectar recipe, 40-41
Nesting, 17-18
Oaks, 32
Ocotillo, *Fouquieria*, **27**
Orioles, as pests, **45**
Penstemons, 29
Plain-capped Starthroat,
   identification of, 61
Plant families, major, 28-31
Plant regions, 25-27
Plant selection, 24-25
Predators, 19
Purple-throated Mountain Gem, **7**
Recycling, 52
Red dye, dangers, 41
Rose of Sharon, *Hibiscus*, **26**
Ruby-throated Hummingbird,
   **10**, **56**
   identification of, 56
Rufous Hummingbird, **11**, **43**, **57**
   identification of, 57
   migration, 11-12
Sages, *Salvia*, **28**
Snakes, 19
Species, number of, 9
Squirrels, as pests, **19**
Sugar water, see Nectar
Sunbirds, **8**
Torpor, 6, 8
Violet-crowned Hummingbird, **60**
   identification of, 60
Wasps, **44**
White-eared Hummingbird, **9**, **60**
   identification of, 60
Xantus's Hummingbird,
   identification of, 61